ITALY monuments past and present

CONTENTS

Text on Rome by A.R. Staccioli; text on Ancient Ostia in collaboration with the Superintendence
of Ostia; text on Hadrian's Villa by C. Morselli; text on Pompeii and Herculaneum by A. De Franciscis,
updating by I.Bragantini; text on Paestum by E. Greco; text on Sicily by G. Messineo

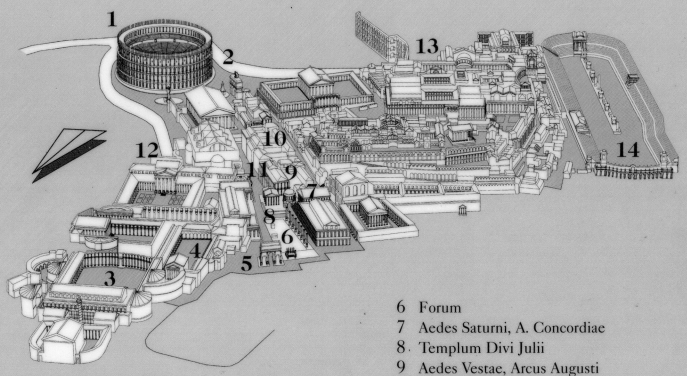

1 Amphiteatrum Flavium
2 Vallis Amphiteatri
3 Forum Traiani, F. Augusti, F. Nervae
4 Forum Julium
5 Forum Romanum

6 Forum
7 Aedes Saturni, A. Concordiae
8 Templum Divi Julii
9 Aedes Vestae, Arcus Augusti
10 Atrium Vestae
11 Templum Divi Romuli
12 Basilica Maxentii
13 Mons Palatinus
14 Circus Maximus

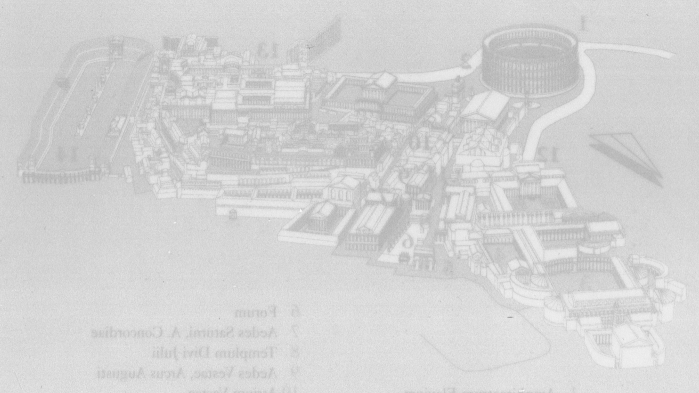

The Palatine Hill boasts the privilege of preserving the most ancient evidence of what was later to become Rome: the rock-hewn floors of two or three huts (which recent archaeological findings suggest were inhabited until the mid 7th century BC) and a burial ground of simple earth graves on the edges of

Ancient Rome

the Roman forum. Of all small villages which sprang up on the hills, separated by broad marshes, the one on the Palatine controlled the Tiber crossing and the market which had long existed on the left bank of the river; so it was that this hill exerted a strong pull on the surrounding centers, which were all incorporated in the 8th and 7th centuries BC, gradually giving rise to the city itself. The latter, even at its point

(left) Trajan's Markets

(right) The House of the Vestal Virgins

of greatest extension, never radically altered its basic layout, the general characteristics of which remained those of the city-state. This was inevitably reflected in the process of the construction of monuments, which was only coordinated when Rome came into contact with the neighboring Etruscan culture (an event which is reflected in legend in the mythical figures of the kings Ancus Marcius, Tarquinius Priscus, Servius Tullius and Tarquinius Superbus, i.e. Tarquin the Proud; indeed, this period is referred to by historians as "the great Rome of the Tarquins".

The city already acquired an *enceinte* of walls in the 6th century BC. Protected by a fortified strong point on the Capitol, it boasted a landing stage on the Tiber and a commercial and political center in the Forum, and it was enriched by public buildings and sanctuaries reflecting the Etruscan influence (most notably, the Temple of Jupiter Optimus Maximus Capitolinus, which legend has it was consecrated by the first consuls of the Republic in 509 BC). Over the course of the next century the city grew to include the Aventine, and in the first half of the fourth century, following recovery from an invasion by the Gauls and the ruin it had left in its wake, a new circle of walls was erected to protect an extensive urban area, now covering over 400 hectares: the biggest city at the time.

After the conquest of the Greek East (2nd-1st centuries BC), entire districts were built or redesigned along the lines of Hellenistic cities: Greek architectural models were adopted, such as the public portico, and new ones were invented, such as the basilica, to house the law courts. These responded better to the pragmatic mentality of the Romans, for whom artistic endeavour was always based on practical requirements. So, in order to better satisfy the needs of the public administration and official representations, architecture became primarily an "art of spaces": each building was

View of the northern slopes of the Palatine: buildings and shops of Neronian age and the arches of the Domus Tiberiana

Base of Trajan's column: detail showing armour and a dragon. Forum Transitorium, south-eastern wall: "le Colonnacce". Detail of Trajan's column

conceived not only on its own terms (as in Classical Greece), but in relation to the surrounding buildings.

The systematic application of arch and vault made it possible to erect ever larger and more functional buildings, such as the commercial porticoes of the vast district known as the Emporium, south of the Aventine. Between 179 and 142 BC, the first stone bridge was built over the Tiber (Pons Aemilius). The Campus Martius (Field of Mars) also started to be developed in the 2nd century, when the first porticoes and temples were erected; Pompey's projects in the next century (porticoes and a theater) made it the city's natural and most important area of expansion.

Under Sulla, previous building materials (wood, the terracotta favored by the Etruscans and stucco-coated tufa) were replaced by travertine or other types of limestone. In the same century, building and town planning became a distinct part of the political program of the heads of state, it being their most valuable instrument of propaganda and self-celebration. Caesar was one of the first to demonstrate this attitude, bequeathing to the city the early stages of a detailed plan of urban development, and the construction of a new forum, the first step in the creation of the monumental complex that the Imperial *fora* were later to become. Under Caesar's successor, Augustus, Rome adopted all the characteristics of the most

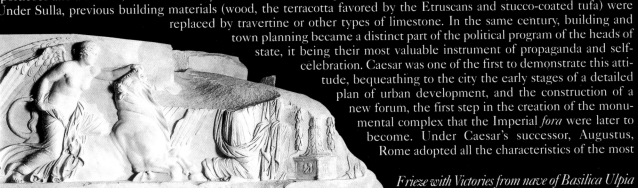

Frieze with Victories from nave of Basilica Ulpia

important Hellenistic cities, to the extent that the Roman emperor was able to boast that he had "found a Rome of terracotta and turned it into marble". Augustus brought to completion many unfinished buildings (such as the Basilica Julia, the Theater of Marcellus and the Curia). He also built another forum, and liberally decorated the Campus Martius with public and private buildings (taking up Caesar's earlier idea), aided by his helpers, first and foremost among whom was Agrippa; these range from the Theater of Balbus to the Amphitheater of Statilius Taurus, from the Baths of Agrippa to the first Pantheon, and from the Altar of Peace (Ara Pacis) to the Augustan Sundial, culminating in the grandiose mausoleum erected for the imperial family. It was also Augustus who, by choosing to live on the Palatine, determined the transformation of the hill into the single, magnificent imperial residence of later years.

After the terrible fire in 64 AD, which razed to the ground ten of the city's fourteen *regiones urbanae*, Nero transformed a good part of the center into a splendid villa, the Domus Aurea (Golden House), and initiated a systematic project for the rebuilding of the city, which can only be said to have been completed under the

The Pantheon

The Mausoleum of Hadrian (Castel Sant'Angelo), night view

The Baths of Caracalla

The Arch of Titus, built to celebrate the triumph of the Emperor for the conquest of Jerusalem

Flavian dynasty, with Domitian's intense building work and after Vespasian and Titus had erected the building which would become the symbol of Rome: the Flavian Amphitheater, or Colosseum (75-80 AD).

The 2nd century AD marked the culmination of construction and urban development in Rome. It is to this period that we may trace Trajan's Baths and Trajan's Forum, the magnificent temples such as that of Venus and Roma, the new Pantheon, the Mausoleum of Hadrian across the Tiber and the two spectacular spiral columns engraved with the exploits of their patrons. Meanwhile in the private sector, multi-storey tenements (*insulae*) were abounding, often forming genuine neighborhoods. In the 3rd century there was a general slowing down of activity, notwithstanding the building of the Baths of Caracalla. In 275 AD Aurelian responded to the growing barbarian menace on the frontiers of the empire by ordering the building of a new circle of city walls, 18km in circumference, which nonetheless contained the greatest, wealthiest and most monumental city hitherto seen on the face of the earth. But building in the city did not come to a complete halt; the Baths of Diocletian and the Basilica of Maxentius, opened by Constantine in 312, constituted two more marvelous chapters in the history of Roman architecture, now spanning over a thousand years. A little later, the Arch of Constantine, erected in his honour by the Senate in 315 with the recycling of material from older monuments was to mark the end of an era. Indeed, Constantinople, which was to be the empire's new capital, the "New Rome", was founded on the shores of the Bosphorus on 11 May 330.

THE COLOSSEUM

The Amphitheatrum Flavium, known universally as the Colosseum, was started by the emperor Vespasian immediately after 70 AD, and inaugurated by his son Titus in 80 AD. The gigantic building occupied the area previously occupied by the artificial lake of the Domus Aurea, in the middle of the valley between the Palatine, the Caelian and the Esquiline.

It was Rome's first permanent amphitheater: an event which was celebrated with a series of ceremonies and spectacles lasting a hundred days, during which 5,000 animals were slaughtered.

Underground areas of the Colosseum

The importance of the event is also underlined by the building's imposing size: the outer circle is almost 50 meters high and the longer axis of the ellipse is 188 meters in diameter (the shorter one is 156 meters). Over 100,000 cubic meters of travertine were employed, along with 300 metric tons of iron for the pins which held the blocks together.

The outer facade, in travertine, presents a triple series of 80 arches which are numbered in sequence (the numbers corresponded to those on the *tesserae* issued to the audience), framed by engaged columns belonging to the three orders and crowned by an attic of Corinthian pilaster strips surmounted by corbels. The audience entered via a concentric series of vaulted corridors, crossed by stairways leading up to the various levels, and thence to the 160 outlets (*vomitoria*).

Next to the Flavian Amphitheater stood the Colossus of Nero (from which the name "Colosseum", used from the Medieval period onwards, is derived). This was a giant statue in gilt bronze, 30 m high, the work of Greek sculptor Zenodoros. It originally represented the emperor, but after his death was modified to depict the sun god.

Inside, the Colosseum had a large, elliptical *arena*, with a wooden floor bearing a bed of sand and covering an area of about 76 m by 46 m. Separated from the arena by a high podium was the *cavea* (seating area), covered entirely in marble, subdivided into three superimposed sectors of steps surmounted by a colonnade (reserved for women), on top of which was a fourth tier of wooden stands providing the standing room for the poorest sections of the public. Indeed, each sector of the cavea was strictly reserved for a particular

Shield, sword and helmet of a Roman legionary (Museo della Civiltà Romana, Rome)

General view of the Via dei Fori Imperiali and the Valley of the Colosseum

class of citizens, the places on top being assigned to the least important, though all enjoyed free entry. Including the standing audience, the amphitheater could accommodate about 70,000 people, who came to watch gladiatorial combats and wild beast hunts as well as less important spectacles of various kinds. An enormous awning protected spectators from the heat of the sun; its segments were hoisted by a special detachment of sailors sent up from the naval base at Misenum, on the Gulf of Naples.

During shows, the arena would be surrounded by a metal mesh carried on poles and spiked with elephant tusks; the top of the mesh was furbished with ivory rollers, to stop the animals from gaining a foothold and escaping from the arena. Just in case, the niches in the podium at the bottom of the cavea were always full of archers, ever ready to intervene.

The last show of which we have certain knowledge was held in 523 AD under Theodoric, King of the Ostrogoths. It consisted only of animal hunts, for gladiator fighting had been abolished in 438 and substituted by these *venationes* (hunts). In the Medieval period it was converted into a castle, and was long used as a quarry for building materials. Despite the continual plundering, it is still the monument of greatest visual impact to survive from Ancient Rome.

The subterranean parts of the Colosseum, probably constructed under Domitian, when it was decided that no further naval battles would be staged, concealed complex technical and construction devices. They contained facilities and stored the stage equipment for the shows: the scenery was often very elaborate, especially for the hunts, when the stage managers did not fight shy of creating hills, woods, and even small lakes.

Real elevators were operated, for men and animals, by means of counterweights. The animals were first driven along the corridors by their handlers and made to enter cages, which were then raised to a higher level, where the cage would open. The animals would thus step out onto a gangway connected to a ramp, with a trap door at the top, from which they would exit into the open, ready for the spectacle. We are told that on one occasion this system was used to bring a hundred lions into the arena at the same moment: their combined roar was so loud that the noisy crowd was frightened into instant silence. The gladiators were able to reach the arena directly from their main barracks (Ludus Magnus), situated next to the Colosseum, by way of an underground passage leading to the amphitheater's underground areas.

THE ROMAN FORUM

The origin of the Forum Romanum is strictly linked to the evolution and transformation into urban structures of the primitive villages which grew up on the higher points of the surrounding hills. Throughout the Republican period, it was the city's commercial, religious, political and legal center. It then became the monumental site of commemoration of Rome's history, right up to the end of the ancient world.

The Valley of the Forum, lying between the Palatine, the Capitol and the first slopes of the Viminal and the Quirinal, must itself have been affected, albeit marginally, by the presence of some modest nuclei of huts and by an extensive burial ground, dating back to the late Bronze age and the early Iron age. Around the end of the 7th century BC, the Cloaca Maxima drained away its stagnant waters and it could thus be formally laid out and receive its first surface.

The Forum Square, reconstruction

From that time onwards, while the north-west part of the Forum, at the foot of the Capitol, was used for public buildings (with the creation of the Comitium, the meeting place of the people's assemblies, and the Curia, the house of the Senate), the broader part took on the role of a public square (the Forum, in the proper sense of the term), with a mixture of commercial and religious buildings. Here were the shops and market places, and also the city's most ancient sanctuaries, dedicated to Vesta, Saturn (guardian of the Aerarium, i.e. the Treasury), Janus, and Castor and Pollux.

The Romans identified a small sanctuary, consisting of an altar, an honorary column and a tufa block with an inscription dating back to the 6th century BC, as the tomb of Romulus, their legendary founder. It was accordingly protected with large slabs of black stone (lapis niger). Another tradition has it that the black cladding was added after the sanctuary had been profaned by the Gauls in the 4th century BC, to mark a place of desecration (*locus funestus*). The Via Sacra crossed the whole length of the square, whence it ascended to the Temple of Jupiter Optimus Maximus on the Capitol.

The construction of the first basilicas in the 2nd century BC (the Porcia, the oldest, the Opimia, the Sempronia, and most importantly the Basilica Aemilia) further emphasized the Forum's character as a political and administrative center, and it gradually assumed its definitive appearance. The stages in this process were: the building of the Tabularium, seat of the state

The Forum Romanum, at night:
in foreground the Temple of Saturn

archives on the northern side (80 BC), providing the square with a monumental backdrop; the moving of the Curia and the Rostra (the platform from which the magistrates addressed the people) and the erection of the Basilica Julia in front of the Basilica Aemilia by Caesar, marking off the long sides of the square; and finally, the positioning of the Temple of Divine Caesar, ordained by Augustus, in order to close off the fourth side of the square.

The structure of the square remained unchanged for a long time. The construction of new buildings, such as the Temple of Vespasian and Titus, underneath the Tabularium, and that of Antoninus and Faustina, built by Antoninus Pius in memory of his wife Faustina, who died in 141 BC, and subsequently dedicated by the Senate to the emperor himself, respected the Augustan layout. The only breach in this convention was the erection of a gigantic equestrian statue of Domitian in the center of the square (this was

later taken down and replaced by one of Constantine). Only from the 3rd century AD onwards was there a new phase of building in the Forum, with the construction of the Arch of Septimius Severus (erected in 202 AD by the Senate and People of Rome in commemoration of an emperor who had extended the frontiers of the Empire as far as Mesopotamia), squeezed in

View of the Basilica Aemilia

Via Sacra: view of the Temple of Divus Julius and of Castor and Pollux ruins

Basilica Aemilia, relief with a bucranium (ox skull)

between the Rostra and the Curia, the seven honorary columns aligned on the south side of the square, in front of the Basilica Julia, and the monuments commemorating the Tetrarchy's tenth anniversary (*decennalia*). Indeed, it fell to one of these columns, the one raised in 608 AD in honour of the Byzantine Emperor Phocas, to become the last monument to be added to the Forum. But by that time the millenary glory of what had once been the most important place in Rome had long since faded away.

THE TEMPLE OF VESTA AND THE ARCH OF AUGUSTUS

The Temple of Vesta, dedicated to the goddess of the "public hearth of the Roman people", stands where the Forum square starts to rise towards the Palatine. It was endowed with particular significance for the Romans, who saw in it the monumental representation of their deep attachment to the values of the domestic sphere, and the guarantee of the survival in time of the history of their city. Indeed, it was here that the Vestal Virgins guarded the sacred and eternal flame, symbol of the eternal life of the city. Stored away in the innermost shrine of this temple and equally jealously guarded, the city also preserved numerous

Golden coin with portrait of Augustus

Marble portrait of the queen Cleopatra

sacred objects (including the Palladium, the wooden image of Pallas Athena) which, as legend would have it, Aeneas had brought from Troy as pledge and warranty of empire. According to some authors, this temple was round in plan because it had originally been built on the model of a hut, the oldest type of hearth and home known in Italy, and had an opening in the roof to let out the smoke generated by the fire.

Aureus with portrait of Antony

It was frequently rebuilt following destruction by fire, the last time in the 2nd century AD by Julia Domna, wife of the Emperor Septimius Severus. Opposite the Temple of Vesta stood the Arch of Augustus, and right in front of this, a small fountain with a circular basin made of white marble. The arch was erected by order of the Senate in 19 BC in order to commemorate the restitution to the emperor of the standards lost by Crassus to the Parthians, and replaced a single-arched structure built in 29 BC to commemorate Augustus's victory over Antony and Cleopatra at Actium in 31 BC. The later structure, which can be reconstructed on the basis of the remains of the foundations and a coin dating 17-15 BC, had three arches: the central one was covered by a vault and the two side ones by architraves. The small aedicules decorating the interior of the smaller arches contained the consular *fasti* (registers of the succession of consuls from

The Temple of Vesta and the Arch of Augustus, reconstruction

the first year of the Republic onwards), while the triumphal *fasti* were carved on the pilasters supporting the architrave, bearing the names of the consuls and generals who had obtained the honour of a triumph, also since early Republican times. At the back, behind the imposing mass of the Temple of Castor and Pollux which stood over the Arch, were the buildings of the Imperial palaces on the Palatine, which looked onto the Forum.

DOMUS AUREA (THE GOLDEN HOUSE OF NERO)

The Domus Aurea stood on the site of the Domus Transitoria, destroyed in the fire of 64 AD. The latter had been ordained by Nero as a continuation of the Julio-Claudian policy of developing the Palatine, which had led to the construction of several *domus*. The gigantic Neronian villa extended from the foot of the Palatine and Caelian to the Gardens of Maecenas on the Esquiline, covering a good hundred hectares. The epithet "golden" suffices to conjure up the magnificence of its decoration and the opulence of its buildings.

The architects engaged on the building of the palace, Severus and Celer, decided to adopt the format, on a colossal scale, of a country villa right in the center of Rome, and the 2nd century historian Tacitus notes that this Domus was admired by people at the time not so much for its precious materials, already seen in the previous palace, as for its woods, meadows and lakes, the largest of which filled the site now occupied by the Colosseum. The buildings therefore covered a vast area extending from the Palatine to the Oppian, at the foot of the Caelian. Suetonius, author of the biographies of the first twelve Caesars, recounts that the *atrium* of the palace consisted of a triple portico which was a thousand paces long (about 1,500 meters) and contained the Colossus, a statue of Nero as sun god, 120 feet high (35 meters).

Coin with the portrait of Nero

The decoration of the interiors made use of all kinds of precious materials: gold and ivory were everywhere, and the flowers in the paintings were set with precious stones. The ceilings of the banqueting halls were fitted with sliding panels of ivory, so that flowers and perfumes could be scattered onto the diners from above. The pictorial decoration, entrusted to the painter Fabullus, was in an opulent, magnificent style, depicting figures framed in geometric patterns endlessly enriched by motifs of plants and imaginary creatures. It is the Oppian Hill sector of this imposing residence that we know best. Built on platforms overlooking the valley in which the Colosseum was later to rise, it was divided into three main blocks. The two lateral ones were based on the traditional nucleus of the peristyle villa, their rooms distributed around a porticoed garden. The central block, separated from the

Portrait of Nero (Museo Nazionale, Rome)

The Domus Aurea, reconstruction

others by large pentagonal gardens, was, on the other hand, built around an octagonal hall, the vault of which was supported by octagonal pillars, with a circular light-well in the center. The sides of the octagon gave onto rectangular rooms, which all looked back towards the center of the hall, where a statue was probably placed, lit to striking effect from the light-well above. This was certainly one of the banqueting halls of the Domus, perhaps the main one which, as Suetonius recounts, rotated continuously on its own axis, like the earth.

After Nero's death in 68 AD, the emperors who succeeded him restored large parts of the Domus Aurea to the city. Public monuments like the Colosseum rose on top of Nero's palace (indeed, it was intended by Vespasian as an act of reparation to assuage the sensibilities of the people, who had been offended by Nero's economic excess and ostentation), along with all the buildings connected to it (e.g. the gladiators' barracks, their hospital and the depot for the stage equipment used during the spectacles), the public baths built by Titus and also the state mint (Moneta).

The last sector to be dismantled was the luxurious Oppian Hill area which, having been stripped of all its recyclable materials, was filled in for the construction of the Baths of Trajan.

Domus Aurea, painting with the representation of Achilles among King Lycomede's daughters, in the palace of Scyros

Ostia was founded as a military colony in the 2nd half of the 4th century BC, in order to control and defend the mouth of the Tiber. This is shown by the early layout of the fortified city as a rectangular *castrum* (194 x 126 m) with walls and gates in tufa. However, there may well

Ancient Ostia

have been an earlier settlement, perhaps located at a junction in the local network of roads, which guarded the movement of traffic up and down the river. Sources also tell us that Ostia was founded by Ancus Marcius, fourth king of Rome, after the destruction of Ficana at the end of the 6th century BC. Ficana was the old Latin town at the mouth of the river (which was much further inland in early historical times

(left) The Theater, cavea

(right) Thermopolium, interior

than it is today). Its conquest was the first and most important step in controlling the riverway.

The site, at Monte Cugno, the ridge overlooking the Tiber to the north of Acilia, is currently under excavation, and is yielding much valuable information on life in the 8th-5th centuries BC. The town of Ostia therefore owed its existence to Rome, i.e. to Rome's position on the Tiber and the expansion of her dominion down to the sea. The fortunes of the capital and her river port were thenceforth tightly interwoven. It is then to Ostia that we may turn in seeking evidence which has been lost in Rome: the pattern of urban development and building techniques (both monumental and functional) which determined the varied fabric of city life.

In fact, the surviving archaeological remains at Ostia represent about the nearest we can come to a typical example of a Roman town. Its history spans some nine hundred years, from the Republic of the 4th century BC to the Late Empire of the 5th century AD.

The city is vast in extension, and it is surrounded by a mighty *enceinte* of walls, protected by towers, witnessing the importance that Ostia acquired between the 3rd and 1st centuries BC, combining its function as an early naval base with that of a center for the distribution of grain to Rome, its army, and all of its territory, as we know from Livy's *Early History of Rome*.

Caesar (Plutarch, *Lives*, Caesar, 58) was the first to express the need for a new and larger harbor, further away from the mouth of the Tiber, which was being

Mosaic floor: lighthouse of Claudian port with merchant ship

Thermopolium sign: painted panel with vegetables

increasingly silted up by sands carried downstream from the tufa areas further north.

However, the project was only undertaken by the emperor Claudius, between 42 and 54 AD, with the construction of a great artificial basin in the area of the modern airport of Fiumicino. Sheltered from the sea by two curving breakwaters, each 800 meters long, the project was finally completed in 105 AD by the emperor Trajan, with the excavation of an inner basin — a huge, hexagonal dry-dock — to extend and supplement the port facilities and enormous monumental warehouses of the Claudian port.

So it was that the Empire of the early 2nd century found Ostia prepared for vast commercial traffic and equally prepared — thanks to the far-sighted Sullan plan — for the boom in civic building which followed. Portus, as the new harbor was called, now handled the heavy shipping, but Ostia still flourished as a rivermouth wharf, and embarked upon the construction of a series of enormous public and private warehouses, the *horrea*, matched by a proliferation of mercantile agencies and administrative offices, all in areas around the forum. Alongside these sprung up premises for those employed in the *annona* (the organization which ensured that the city received an adequate food supply) and its network of associated services, and for itinerant traders, merchants, manufacturers, associations of artisan craftsmen, lawyers and brokers; indeed, the very world from which there arose a new social phenomenon: what we might now loosely term a middle class.

Ostia offers a unique view of that society, a fascinating glimpse of what Rome herself must have been like at the height of her magnificence. It ran the full gamut of Roman social history. It saw the old single-family *domus* evolve into a living-intensive block, the *insula*, as the formation of classes of laborers and free craftsmen gave rise to small modular apartments in larger multi-storeyed buildings. Both private homes and civil and religious public buildings were decorated with very fine mosaics and wall decorations. A favorite color for walls was a warm, golden yellow, frequently enlivened with scenes associated with the sea: Aphrodite, for example, rising from the waves amid leaping dolphins. Others were drawn from rural life. Occasionally we discover clients with a taste for literary or mythological subjects — tales from Homer,

Greengrocer's sign

such as that of Ulysses and the Sirens — while yet others chose allegorical themes, featuring the Muses or the Graces. The latter turn up in marble form as well, little sculptures enlivening gardens and fountains, and sometimes appear among the variety of elements brightening the austerity of a tomb.

The continual transition of outsiders and the city's pleasant location on the coast, surrounded by a pine forest and the Mediterranean *maquis*, may help explain the large number of bathing establishments (*thermae*) in Ostia (as many as 12) and the introduction of the cults of oriental divinities such as Cybele, Attis, Isis, Serapis and especially the little Persian god of light, Mithras. No ancient city has as yet proved so rich in *mithraea*. Some fourteen of these special shrines have come to light so far: small chapels furnished with two wide stone dining-couches, where Mithras's slaying of the bull was celebrated in ritual banquets, the meat tranferring the divine purification of the victim's blood onto the participants. Ostia is a marvelous illustration of this transition from old world to new: a strong nucleus of Christianity flourished alongside all the other cult activities, and the Jewish community ran a synagogue with its services. It was in Ostia that the Christians buried their first martyrs, victims of persecution in 269 AD.

Ostia maintained a position of such prestige at the Imperial court that Maxentius, as prefect of Rome in 309, accorded it the benefit of a mint to coin currency in commemoration of his father Maximian and young son Romulus, both recently deceased. After Maxentius's defeat and the definitive victory of his adversaries, Constantine also took a particular interest in Portus and Ostia, providing the former with a strong defensive wall, and the latter with the first official monument to Christianity, with the dedication of a large basilica to the Saints Peter, Paul and John the Baptist. From then on it was the Bishop of Ostia who consecrated the Pope as Bishop of Rome, and the city was honored with a number of prestigious monuments linked to this new religious authority. From one of these, left incomplete in the mid-4th century, excavations have recovered the unique image of Christ blessing, set in a rich decoration of inlaid marble (Museum of Ostia Antica).

WALKING IN THE ANCIENT CITY

The itinerary through the site which begins at Porta Romana and the city's Decumanus Maximus can be extended east to the Porta Laurentina, or west, to the banks of the Tiber. Heading towards the sea, to the south, we reach Porta Marina and the coastal area, along which runs the Via Severiana and which is scattered with baths and villas. For the purposes of this visit, the city may be divided into five *regiones*: the first comprises the area around the Forum, which only acquired a truly monumental aspect in the Imperial age.

The Capitolium constitutes the heart of the forum. This was Ostia's most important temple, dedicated to the Capitoline triad. It is a hexastyle building (i.e. with 6 columns across the front), standing on a high platform, and was built under the emperor Hadrian on the site of a Republican-age temple. In front of the Capitolium stands the Temple of Augustus and Rome, also hexastyle, on a platform, with two flights of steps at the sides. This was an Imperial sanctuary, created to celebrate the cult of the emperor and the grandeur of Rome; indeed, inside was a statue of Rome as Victory, dressed as an Amazon. On the west side of the square stands the Basilica, which covered about 1000 square meters. This was the place

Forum and Capitolium

for business transactions and court hearings, where litigation resolved. At the far south-east of the Forum stands the large complex of the Forum Baths (*thermae*). Built around the mid-2nd century AD, they remained in use over a long period, and were rebuilt and embellished on several occasions.

The second region is dominated by the Theater. This was built under Augustus and restored on several occasions. Its groundplan and foundations are still well-preserved, but the elevated parts of the portico and cavea have been reconstructed in modern restorations. Separated from the theater by just the stage wall was the Piazzale delle Corporazioni Marittime (Square of the Guilds), the center of the city's economic life (as witnessed by the many mosaic pavements of a commercial or maritime nature), with its large portico which must have doubled as a shelter for theatergoers in case of rain. Further on stood the Baths of Neptune (really large public baths, so called due to the grandiose mosaic in the entrance hall portraying Neptune drawn by four sea-horses). Started under Hadrian in 133 AD, they were completed under Antoninus Pius. Further on we reach the Caserma dei Vigili (firemen's barracks), a building of considerable proportions, created to house a corps of firemen first posted to Ostia from the Roman garrisons by order of the emperor Claudius some time in the mid-1st century AD.

The third region contains the area of the Republican sanctuaries, notable among which is the Temple of Hercules, which dates back to the first half of the 1st century BC. This is a hexastyle building with a tufa colonnade of Tuscan order. There follows the area used for commercial purposes, with its large warehouses (*horrea*) and its multi-storey apartment blocks.

The fourth region consists of the Schola Traiana, a building with a porch facing onto the Decumanus, its circular *exedra* featuring large fountains decorated with niches. It was built in the 2nd century AD on top of private dwellings of Augustan date, for the meetings and banquets of one of Ostia's wealthy corporations.

Finally, the fifth region features large examples of industrial architecture, such as fullers' workshops and mills, and also baths, *mithraea* and private dwellings.

The Museo Ostiense is located on the site's premises. On display are some 600 pieces of sculpture, drawn from the 3,000

Detail of mosaic floor in the Baths of Neptune

A stretch of the Decumanus. Small market. Macellum, fishmonger's shop

or more which make up the actual collection, and a wide variety of other finds. Much of the material has come and is still coming from the necropolis on the Isola Sacra, but nevertheless affords intimate reflections of the everyday life of Ostia's ancient inhabitants. The inscriptions, currently numbering over 9,000, give us the names and careers of generations of Ostians themselves, city magistrates and officials, successful merchants and members of the most diverse trades and professions. The *amphorae* and vases recall the presence of the most celebrated wines, the best Spanish olive oil and the famous fish sauces (*garum*); little alabaster and glass paste bottles call up the aroma of balsamic oils and spices from the East. Chalices, cups, bronzes, and finely wrought lanterns of varying form and decoration bear witness to the elegance of Ostia's tables and the refinement of detail in the furnishing of its houses and buildings, the intimate details of human life.

FIREMEN'S BARRACKS

This building, built under Hadrian in around 130 AD, was restored by Septimius Severus and Caracalla in the first decades of the 3rd century AD. It was created to house a cohort of firemen posted from the Roman garrisons, set up in Ostia by order of the emperor Claudius in around the middle of the 1st century AD in order to combat the numerous fires which were frequently destroying warehouses and the food supplies stored in them.

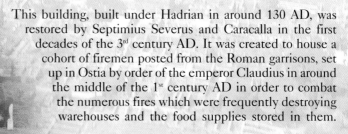

Square of the Guilds
The Firemen's Barracks, reconstruction

Organized on a military basis, the cohort of *vigiles* also kept an eye on activity at the harbor, formed a Night Watch and lent a hand in the frequent battles against Tiber floods.

The barrack building, originally constructed on two floors, of which only the first survives, is a notable piece of Hadrianic architecture. It consists of an open porticoed courtyard (70 by 41 meters), with rooms on the north, east and south wings. On the west side, facing the entrance and preceded by a vestibule with a sacrificial scene on the mosaic floor, is an Augusteum, a chapel for the worship of the emperor and his family. Still in place on the platform where the ceremonies were held is a row of bases with dedicatory inscriptions to various emperors. In the south-west corner of the building there is a latrine and a shrine to Fortuna Sancta.

THE THERMOPOLIUM BUILDING

The Thermopolium building is the one at the end of Via di Diana, on the left (coming from Via dei Molini). It largely repeats the general characteristics of any rented block. Worthy of note is the external balcony borne on travertine slabs (a similar one has been reconstructed in glazed concrete on the next building) and the Thermopolium (snack bar) on the ground floor. There were a large number of snack bars, wine bars and public eating places in Ostia, much used by the local

1st century BC relief with market scene (Museum of Ostia Antica)

Relief with warship (Pio-Clementino Museum, Vatican)

Wine amphorae, the cargo of a sunken ship

The Thermopolium reconstruction

Headquarters of the Augustales

workers and passing customers of the most varied origin, coming into Ostia with the cargo ships.

The spacious premises of this Thermopolium faced onto the street, with three large openings onto the outside, of which two are stone benches.

The interior was divided into three rooms, of which the middle one was the main one, with its sales-counter lined in marble slabs and fitted with two sinks, and a kind of display case with shelves on which the food was displayed; a painting depicts the usual fare: pickled eggs, grapes, olives and a radish. One of the side rooms was used as a kitchen, while the other, smartened in appearance due to the color of the walls and a mosaic pavement, may have been a saloon for clients of higher rank or at any rate more leisure.

Reconstruction of a large apartment building in Ostia (Rome, Museo della Civiltà Romana)

The villa is located on a small plain on the slopes of the Tiburtine Hills to the southeast of Tivoli (*Tibur*), a town not far from Rome which combines a pleasant climate with a pretty and peaceful landscape, enlivened by hills and valleys. The site chosen for the Imperial residence

Hadrian's Villa

was previously occupied by a villa of Republican age (late 2nd-early 1st century BC), which may have been inherited by the emperor's wife, Vibia Sabina. The later complex was developed out of this older nucleus, which was incorporated into Hadrian's project. Contemporary literary sources are virtually silent as to the historical and artistic importance of Hadrian's creation. The biographer of the *Historia*

(left) The northern side of the Canopus

(right) The "Maritime Theater"

Augusta mentions that the emperor chose to call the various parts of the villa after the famous places and monuments he had visited while touring the provinces: the Stoa Poikile (painted porch), the Academy, the Prytaneum and the Lyceum in Athens; the Vale of Tempe in Thessaly; and the Canopus in Egypt. So these names came to be attributed to the various buildings in the complex by scholars over the centuries, on a somewhat arbitrary basis (with the exception of the Canopus), but they are still used to this day. What the paragraph in question does reflect is Hadrian's great passion for travel, which led him to tour the vast territories of the Empire, of which he was not only a tireless admirer — attracted as he was by the beauty of nature and traditions of humanity — but also a careful organizer. Also groundless is the legend, fueled by a passage by the 4th century historian Aurelius Victor, according to which the villa was built in the emperor's dotage: it was actually built in the early years of his reign. A detailed study of the buildings has given us precise dates as regards their age, with the identification of two dis-

Detail of the statue of Hermes from the Canopus

Heliocaminus Baths

tinct phases of construction, interrupted only by the emperor's grand tours of the provinces. The first was between the years 118 and 125 AD, and the second was from 125 to 133 AD. However, the swift execution of the project suggests that it was already finalized in precedence, and that Hadrian himself was responsible for its development. Indeed, sources relate that the emperor loved to dabble in architecture and the sciences and insisted on playing a major role in architectural decisions and the solving of technical problems. The historian Dion Cassius recounts a violent quarrel with the famous Apollodorus of Damascus, Trajan's chief architect, whose unveiled criticism of Hadrian's projects was to cost him his life.

When the emperor left on his first journey across the Empire in 121 AD, the Republican villa had already been incorporated into the Imperial palace and the Teatro Marittimo, the neighboring Sala dei Filosofi (Philosophers' Hall) and the Terme con Eliocamino had all been completed. The Stoa Poikile (Pecile), the Nymphaeum (Stadio) and adjoining complexes, and the Small and Great Thermae were all completed during his absence. Many projects were already underway before his second departure in 128 AD: the Greek and Latin Libraries, the Accademia, the Ospitali and the Cento Camerelle. These were followed by the large *triclinium* complexes of the Piazza d'Oro and the Canopus. When Hadrian finally returned in 134 AD, the villa was complete. Small restorations and limited alterations suggest that the complex continued to be used after Hadrian's death. However, his successors preferred to reside in Rome, and the Tiburtine villa was used only for vacations.

Abandoned and stripped of its works of art as early as the 3rd century AD, it was gradually forgotten.

Portrait of the emperor Hadrian

THE EMPEROR HADRIAN

Hadrian was of Iberian origin, as was his predecessor and tutor, Trajan, who adopted him shortly before his death. He was proclaimed emperor in 117 AD, at the age of forty. "He was tall in stature and elegant in appearance; he had silky hair and wore a full beard to cover up the natural blemishes on his face; and he was also very strongly built. He rode and walked a great deal, and always kept himself in training with arms and the javelin. He was at the same time severe and jovial, affable and austere, passionate and contained, niggardly and generous, candid and artful, cruel and merciful". So the late biographer of the *Historia Augusta* (4th century AD) describes the physical appearance and character of Hadrian, a man of a complex personality. This authoritarian and ambitious Spaniard proved to be a talented, refined and enlightened organizer of the Empire, which he governed for twenty years. He was a careful administrator of the state apparatus, renewing appointments and functions, creating a decentralized judicial system and developing the role of public officials for the control of public finances. He made several visits to the provinces, where he promoted a policy of abandoning those territories regarded as impossible to defend (such as Armenia, Assyria and Mesopotamia), and outlined a new frontier defense system. The *vallum* (rampart) which he built in Britannia, since known as Hadrian's Wall, is certainly the most complete and noteworthy defense system of the whole Roman age. He was therefore a man of peace, and promoted projects of urban development and construction, aimed at consolidating and encouraging the spread of Roman civilization. He founded new cities in Egypt, Asia Minor and Thrace, and he built new roads and bridges in Gaul. A lover of Greece, he did his best to rescue the province's economy, and funded important public works in Athens.

In Rome, too, the age of Hadrian was a period of very intensive building, with the construction of projects of great architectural significance (such as the Pantheon, the Temple of Venus and Rome, and his own mausoleum, now the Castel Sant'Angelo), blending Classical traditions and new patterns. Such was the style of all architecture under Hadrian, one of the most complete expressions of which is Hadrian's Villa. Hadrian died in 138 AD, at the age of sixty-two, after appointing Antoninus Pius as his successor.

In 1450, after many centuries of oblivion, during which the site was used as a quarry for bricks and marble, the imposing and suggestive ruins were finally identified as Hadrian's Villa.

LAYOUT AND ARCHITECTURE

The complex covers an area of about 120 hectares and now appears as a beautiful park, scattered with monumental and apparently isolated blocks of buildings facing in different directions. However, we can identify four main axes: Torre di Roccabruna, the Canopus, the Stoa Poikile (Pecile) and the Piazza d'Oro.
The Roccabruna complex includes a building with a tower (possibly a belvedere, as it provides a splendid view), built on a square plan with a monumental entrance arch leading into an octagonal inner hall. Connected to the tower by a substructure is the Accademia, which was a reception area, consisting of a peristyle off which there were a large room and a round hall enlivened by engaged columns in brick, containing alternating rectangular and semicircular niches. A long cryptoporticus links this complex to that of the Piazza d'Oro, which was probably an enormous, luxurious reception area for parties, with gardens and fountains and equipped for banquets, with a capacity for hundreds of

The Building of the Three Exedrae

guests. The plan and architecture are extraordinarily original, with extremely elaborate and structurally sophisticated spatial divisions; there was a large, octagonal vestibule (topped by a beautiful "umbrella" cupola), which led into a large, internal peristyle, from which there developed an intricate system of rooms.

The axis of the Stoa Poikile (Pecile) is set by an immense, rectangular, colonnaded square with rounded sides, roofed colonnades and a fishpond, off which lies a *triclinium* (dining hall) and a nymphaeum in the form of a stadium.

The substructures known as the Cento Camerelle (hundred chambers) connect this complex to that of the Canopus, undoubtedly one of the villa's most original and spectacular features. Situated in a small valley, it has a long channel of water down the middle, a curved short north end, and a Corinthian colonnade down the sides bearing an alternation of arched and flat architraves. To the south of the channel is a large, rectangular piscina, and at the end of the valley is a monumental nymphaeum with a semicircular *exedra*. The whole is decorated with a vast quantity of sculptures, which are copies and reworkings of Greek originals.

A recent and picturesque interpretation sees the Canopus as the symbolic representation of the course of the Nile: the long corridor is the river, the cascades are the cataracts and the large channel is the Mediterranean, with Ephesus to the east (symbolized by statues of Amazons) and Athens to the west (represented by Caryatids). The enormous extension of Hadrian's Villa, its quantity of buildings and the originality and complexity of its architectural forms make it a unique monument in the history of ancient architecture.

The perfect fusion of architectural structures and rolling park gardens is only apparently casual; actually, it is the fruit of a careful study of the sites and a thorough search for landscaping effects, which deeply alter the natural morphology of the site and bend it to the requirements of precise spatial and structural plans. The result is a harmonious and integrated whole of carefully planned buildings. Everything is grandiose and painstakingly calculated. Not only is it the permanent residence of the emperor, his palace for receptions, to be used for official ceremonies, festivities, banquets, and spectacles for the more important guests, it is

Statue of Caryatid from the Canopus

also a place of retreat, stillness and tranquillity. Nothing is casual, either in the reception areas or in the plainer rooms and service areas. Everything is carefully planned, with special attention to routes.

An underground network of carriageways and walkways was even created, so that the traffic of all the vehicles and personnel servicing the villa — certainly heavy, given its size and functions — would not interfere with the main surface routes, which were for official and ceremonial use only, keeping them free of noise, dust and obstruction.

Hadrian's Villa was the site of an architectural experiment where consolidated aspects of the Roman tradition were reworked in new and original combinations. The villa contains an exceptional variety of architectural forms, all characterized by a taste for monumental size, landscaping, the use of multi-linear themes in both horizontal and vertical plans, and complex outlines for the domes and vaults. This is derived from the endless combination and reworking of a few basic elements (porticoes, *exedrae* and rectangular, square and circular halls).

ISLAND VILLA

The name given to this singular building ("maritime theater") was completely fanciful. Circular in plan, it was surrounded by a high outer wall which secluded it from nearby buildings. Inside, a circular portico with marble columns and a barrel vault is separated

Statue from the Canopus

Island Villa, reconstruction

from a small circular island by a moat. On the island stands a miniature villa, originally reached across two wooden drawbridges, later replaced by the current stone bridge.

A semicircular vestibule with side corridors led into a small peristyle with concave sides and a central fountain, with several rooms opening off it. On the south side was a *tablinum* (living room), with two symmetrical adjoining rooms (perhaps rest rooms). On the west side was a small bath building, with *apodyterium* (dressing room), *frigidarium* (cold room, containing a cold plunge-bath and steps down to the moat), *caldarium* (hot room) and a latrine. On the east side was a suite of rooms, perhaps for a library. This small, charming Island Villa, the plan of which may have been based on a moated building in the Palace of Dionysius the Elder in Syracuse, was probably used by the emperor as a private summer residence. Fitted with all the amenities for comfortable living, it offered security and privacy, making it the ideal place for secluded retreat.

BUILDING OF THE CRYPTOPORTICUS AND FISHPOND AND THE NYMPHAEUM-STADIUM

Even though located on different levels and built in different periods, these two buildings belong to a single, enormous complex which also comprises the Building of the three Exedrae (recently identified as the emperor's winter residence). The Building of the Cryptoporticus and Fishpond is built on three levels. The living quarters proper were on the upper one, with large halls which were heated and richly decorated. The fishpond, on this level, was purely ornamental, and decorated with statues and surrounded by a large portico of 40 columns. On the

Statue of Old Centaur from Hadrian's Villa

The Nymphaeum-Stadium, reconstruction

middle level were service rooms and passageways, and a four-sided cryptoporticus, one of the best preserved in the whole villa, leading to corridors and stairways which gave access to the other floors. Its walls were coated in plaster and frescoed: on them we may still read the scratched names of those visitors and artists arriving in the 17th and 18th centuries, some of them famous, e.g. Piranesi. On the ground floor were several rooms, some richly decorated, leading directly to the Nymphaeum (Stadio).

These may have been reception areas and monumental entrance halls.

Recent excavations carried out in the stadium-shaped building have shown that it was actually a large Nymphaeum, divided into three sectors. The north part was entered via a long garden with porticoes on three sides and basins for water and plants. It was occupied by three adjacent rooms. In the center, there was an open area with porticoes on two sides, which connected with the buildings on either side. The south part had an open-air pavilion borne up by columns and surrounded by a moat. At the end was a large fountain with an *exedra*-like plan: water cascaded down the steps of the half circle and flowed through small channels into the basin in front.

Island Villa, *detail of peristyle*

Pompeii stands on a lava spur which juts out into the plain from the slopes of Vesuvius, a short distance from the sea and from the River Sarno. Since earliest times, its advantageous geographical position had always attracted human settlement and favored the

Pompeii

development of agricultural and commercial activities.

In historical times, the Campanian city occupied a perfect position on the chequerboard of Southern Italy, which was dominated first by the Greeks, and then by the Etruscans, so that it was able to borrow from the culture and art of both civilizations.

It fell under Samnite domination in 424 BC, and from this time on we

(left) The Forum Square

(right) Peristyle of the House of Meleager, with a marble pool in the middle

have more knowledge of the city's layout and development. In the period immediately after the Samnite wars, Pompeii entered the Roman orbit as an allied city, an alliance to which it remained faithful even during the Punic wars. It preserved its administrative and linguistic autonomy right up to the end of the 2nd century BC, but it was finally sacked and subjugated by Sulla in 89 BC, for having taken part in the Social War against Rome.

In 80 BC it became a Roman colony, known as "Colonia Cornelia Veneria Pompeianorum". Henceforth its history forms part of the larger picture of Roman history. The only local episode of note, mentioned by the historian Tacitus, is a riot in the amphitheater between the inhabitants of Pompeii and Nuceria (in AD 59), which led to the suspension of all shows for a period of ten years, by senatorial decree.

Pompeii was badly damaged by the earthquake which hit Campania in AD 62 and the damage had not been entirely repaired when, in AD 79, an eruption of Vesuvius killed many of its inhabitants and buried the whole city beneath a rain of ash and fragments of pumice stone (*lapilli*). A graphic description of the disaster is given in two letters by Pliny the Younger to Tacitus, describing among other things the rescue work undertaken by his uncle, Pliny the Elder, who was then commander of the Roman fleet at Misenum and paid for his altruistic initiative with his life. Pompeii never rose from its ruins and the site was virtually abandoned. The first signs of the buried city only came to light many centuries later, and by total chance, when the architect Domenico Fontana was constructing an aqueduct in the Contrada Civita to channel the waters of the river Sarno, between 1594 and 1600.

The fortuitous discovery was not followed up by any archaeological investigation; this only took place in 1748, under the Bourbons (whose reign was marked by intense archaeological activity throughout Southern Italy), when they opened a proper dig which has been underway ever since. Obviously, the system of excavation has not always been the same over the last 250 years, during which there have been significant changes and developments in the science of archaeology itself. Initially, only the finding of objects of artistic importance was regarded as being worthy of interest, but now the remains of material culture have also acquired scientific dignity and become the object of systematic study. And the exceptional circumstances in which Pompeii was buried, ceasing to exist within the exceedingly brief span of two days, enable the scholar to explore a reality — that of everyday life in the ancient world — which historians and archaeologists are hardly ever able to reconstruct with such precision. Thanks also to the ingenious method devised by archaeologist Giuseppe Fiorelli (of recovering the shapes of buried organic material by pouring plaster into the hollows left after their decomposition), the ancient city has come down to us virtually unaltered, throwing light on many aspects of the culture and customs of the time. Indeed, only in Pompeii may we observe such a rich variety of examples of the evolution of Italic and Roman houses and their painted decoration, from the 2nd century BC to the 1st century AD. Another important contribution is that made by Pompeii's scratched and painted graffiti to our knowledge of the manners, institutions and spoken language of the Roman world in the 1st century AD. As for its monuments, the city appears as it was in its final phase of development, surrounded by walls with defense towers and entrance gates. Its layout can best be understood by following three different itineraries.

The first itinerary, in the south-west sector, leads straight through the Porta Marina to the city center, the Forum. The latter is a big, rectangular square, the short north side of which is occupied by the Temple of Jupiter.

Hexastyle (i.e. with 6 columns across the front), Corinthian and built on a high base (in around the 2nd century BC), it was only later converted by the Romans into the Capitolium. The south-east corner of the Forum was used for political functions, as indicated by the three buildings of Imperial date (one of which has been recognized as the Curia, the seat of the Senate) and the Comitium (the place where citizens gathered to elect public officials).

The oldest buildings, notably the Temple of Apollo, were on the west side, which was not affected by the extensive alterations undertaken during the Imperial period. These mainly affected the east side, where the Building of Eumachia, headquarters of

Cast of a victim of the Vesuvius eruption

The Last Day of Pompeii
(by K.P. Bruelow 1799-1853
St. Petersburg, Russian State Museum)

Relief with sacrificial scene from the altar of Temple of Vespasian in the Forum

the Corporation of the *fullones* (fullers and wool launderers), was erected in the reign of Tiberius (so-called after the name of the priestess who dedicated it to Concordia Augusta and Pietas); the erroneously named Temple of Vespasian, actually dedicated to the imperial cult, was also built in this period. At a short distance away from the Forum stood the Temple of Fortuna Augusta, dating back to the early years of the Empire. This itinerary also enables us to follow the evolution of the Pompeian house, as well as that of public and sacred buildings: indeed, the House of the Faun (2nd century BC) is a reflection of the period in which the Samnite aristocracy was first being educated to the tastes of Greek art and culture, and the House of the Vettii (1st century AD) represents the final period of luxury private homes and mercantile affluence. This first itinerary may be concluded with a visit to the bathing establishments (the Thermae of the Forum and the Thermae Stabianae), the theaters (the Teatro Grande and the Odeion) and the places of pleasure (including the Lupinar, one of Pompeii's five brothels).

The second itinerary runs along the part of Pompeii's Decumanus Inferior leading from the Forum to the Porta di Sarno, which is known as the Via dell'Abbondanza; this was probably the city's main artery, as it runs along its entire length, connecting the main centers of the city: the Forum, the theater area and the Amphitheater, with its Great Palaestra. The amphitheater is one of the oldest to have survived (80-70 BC); the *cavea* had a capacity for an audience of 20,000.

The Temple of Fortuna Augusta

House of the Vettii, detail of the garden

House of the Vettii, detail of the triclinium decoration

House of the Vettii, Cupids making perfumes

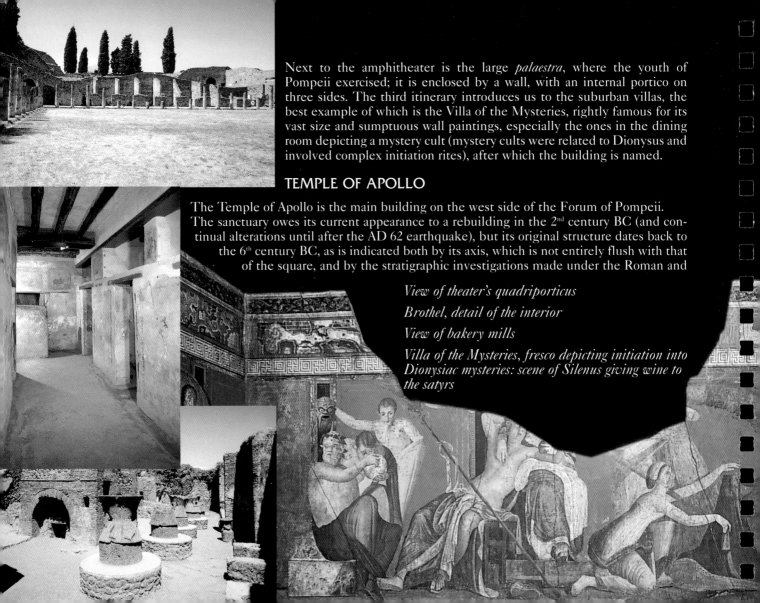

Next to the amphitheater is the large *palaestra*, where the youth of Pompeii exercised; it is enclosed by a wall, with an internal portico on three sides. The third itinerary introduces us to the suburban villas, the best example of which is the Villa of the Mysteries, rightly famous for its vast size and sumptuous wall paintings, especially the ones in the dining room depicting a mystery cult (mystery cults were related to Dionysus and involved complex initiation rites), after which the building is named.

TEMPLE OF APOLLO

The Temple of Apollo is the main building on the west side of the Forum of Pompeii. The sanctuary owes its current appearance to a rebuilding in the 2nd century BC (and continual alterations until after the AD 62 earthquake), but its original structure dates back to the 6th century BC, as is indicated both by its axis, which is not entirely flush with that of the square, and by the stratigraphic investigations made under the Roman and

View of theater's quadriporticus

Brothel, detail of the interior

View of bakery mills

Villa of the Mysteries, fresco depicting initiation into Dionysiac mysteries: scene of Silenus giving wine to the satyrs

Samnite levels. The sacred precinct is bounded by a wall with porticoes on three sides, the columns of which were originally Ionic, bearing a Doric frieze of metopes and triglyphs. After the earthquake of AD 62, the columns were altered to Corinthian with a stucco facing, now completely lost, and the frieze was made continuous, and decorated with gryphons and festoons of leaves. The Fourth Style wall paintings also belong to this period, with scenes from the Trojan wars, though only very few traces remain; in front of the portico there were herms of Mercury and statues of gods, including bronze ones of Apollo and Diana.

The temple stands towards the back of the courtyard, on a high podium with steps up the front. The *cella* was fairly small, but contained an opulent lozenge-and-meander floor decoration in colored stones and slate. Here was the cult statue and navel stone (*omphalos*), an attribute of Apollo.

In front of the temple, in the middle of the open space, is a simple altar of Greek marble on a travertine base; and beside the steps, a column bearing a dedicatory inscription and surmounted by a sundial was added in the Augustan age. The worship of Apollo in this temple may also have been associated in some way with that of the emperor Augustus, who was particularly devoted to this god, under whose protection he won the battle of Actium against Antony and Cleopatra in 31 BC.

HOUSE OF THE FAUN

This is the largest and finest house in Pompeii (occupying some 3,000 m², almost the space of an entire *insula*). It is noteworthy for the dignity of its architecture, the sober refinement of its First Style wall decoration, in squares of polished stucco imitating slabs of variegated marble, and for the high quality of its mosaics (now exhibited at the Naples Archaeological Museum). Such opulence is a clear indication of the considerable economic resources enjoyed by the Italic aristocracies. The pavement in front of the front door bears the greeting *ave*; high on the walls in the entrance hall are two temple-shaped *lararia*; then there is a spacious *atrium tuscanicum* featuring a large, central *impluvium*.

The latter is decorated with a statuette of a dancing Faun, the fine Hellenistic artefact of the 3rd-2nd centuries BC after which the house has

Bronze statue of Apollo in the pose of an archer

House of the Faun, reconstruction

been named (the original is in the Museum of Naples). Opening off the atrium are the bedrooms and, at the far end, the *tablinum* and two dining rooms, one for winter use, with a mosaic of fish and seafood, and the other for autumn, with Dionysus riding a panther. To the right of the atrium is another living area, with its own atrium, the roof of which is borne on four Ionic columns, and service areas (kitchen, bathroom, toilet, etc.).

At the far end of the first large peristyle garden are two more dining rooms, for spring and summer use, and a large hall with a pavement portraying the Battle of Alexander, a magnificent composition based on the work of one of the greatest Greek artists, with a Nile scene on the threshold. There follows a second, much larger *peristylum*, with a two-storeyed Doric portico. The house also had an upper storey, of which little is left. The House of the Faun was built in the 2nd century BC, in the Samnite period, and shows how strong Hellenistic influence was on the Italic architecture of the time. This emerges most clearly in the double peristyle, and also in the great importance attributed to the rooms designed for *otium* (leisure) and dining; this type of house went on to become very fashionable, contributing to the evolution of luxury homes and seaside villas in the Imperial period.

As with the majority of the houses in Pompeii, we do not know the name of the family who lived in it, but it must have been one of the most important families of Pompeii's Samnite period. It should therefore be stressed that the house retained its original decorations right up to the end of the city's life (in particular its sumptuous mosaic decoration, to which subtle allegorical meanings have been attributed), apparently surviving a period which was certainly one of great turmoil in the life of Pompeii, i.e. that of the Social War and the consequent reduction to colony status in the year 80 BC.

THE MAIN THEATER

Pompeii had two theaters, a smaller, roofed *odeion* (auditorium) for recitations, musical performances and pantomimes, and the real theater, which was larger and open, but could be covered with an awning if necessary. Its current appearance dates back to its last rebuilding in the 1st century BC (the *frons scaenae* is the only part which may post-date the AD 62 earthquake). It had undergone many phases of construction: when first erected on the slopes of the acropolis (occupied by the forum buildings) in the late 3rd century BC, it featured open *parodoi* (side entrances through which the actors appeared), a tempo-

Bronze statuette of dancing Faun

The Main Theater, reconstruction

rary stage building and tiered seating in limestone. At the end of the next century, when the whole city was transformed along Italic-Hellenistic criteria, a rectilinear stage front with five doors was added. A few years after the reduction of Pompeii to a Roman colony, the stage building was adapted to classic form: the *pulpitum* (stage platform) was brought forward, and the stage front was moved back. The theater acquired its definitive form under Augustus, when the seating area was cased in marble under the supervision of architect Marcus Artorius Primus. The upper part (*summa cavea*) is raised on a vaulted corridor (*crypta*) and the middle and lower areas (*media* and *ima cavea*) rest directly on the ground, with the *tribunalia* for distinguished spectators set over the entrances to the orchestra. The building held about 5,000 spectators. The orchestra, no longer used by actors and chorus, was also available for seating, probably for citizens of the upper classes. There was a low stage platform, of Roman type; the stage front contained niches and aedicules, with three doorways simulating the facade of a building. Behind, was the actors' dressing room and next to it, a square area with colonnades all around: the *porticus post scaenam*, where the audience would mill in intervals between shows or during bad weather. A group of inscriptions found in the theater commemorate the work of M. Artorius Primus, mentioned above, and also the munificence of the two distinguished citizens who paid for it, M. Holconius Rufus and M. Holconius Celer.

The *velarium* (awning) that gave shade to the building was supported by pilasters built into the wall of the *summa cavea*. It was hoisted and trimmed as required by means of a system of ropes and pulleys. The velarium covering the stage front functioned in a similar manner.

Odeion, internal view

Herculaneum was supposedly founded on the slopes of Vesuvius by Hercules. Initially in the political orbit of the nearby Greek colonies (Cumae and Neapolis, in particular), it was later dominated by the Samnites in the 5th century BC. Like Pompeii, it took part in the Social War

Herculaneum

against Rome, and so was sacked in 89 BC and reduced to the status of *municipium*. In AD 62, it suffered serious damage in the earthquake which devastated so much of Campania, and in AD 79 the little town was also victim of the eruption of Vesuvius. However, instead of being buried in a rain of ash and fragments of pumice stone (*lapilli*), it was overwhelmed by clouds of scorching toxic gas, alter-

(left) Peristyle of the House of Telephus

(right) The Forum Baths, the colonnaded palaestra

nating on at least six occasions with torrents of volcanic mud, which swept away people, objects and buildings, even tearing off the roofs of houses. This gradually buried the city, covering it entirely and solidifying into a compact shelf of rock, similar to tufa in appearance and consistency. On this occasion alone, the ground level rose by an average of about 20 meters. The same flows, upon reaching the sea, caused the coast line to advance by some 450 meters and also created a tidal wave. After the eruption, the emperor Titus sent two commissioners to the site, with instructions to appropriate the property of heirless victims, in order to compensate the stricken survivors. Ancient sources and findings from excavations do seem to indicate that the site was reoccupied later on in antiquity, at least in part.

Unlike Pompeii, Herculaneum features a remarkable continuity of the Italic tradition (in its Samnite form) in its culture and buildings. Its economy must have been based mainly on agriculture and fishing, which also determined the social make-up: what we find is a mixture of humble classes and families of distinguished lineage. Systematic excavations only began in 1738, after a few random finds, by order of King Charles III of Bourbon; so the ancient city gradually came back to the light.

The plan of Herculaneum appears to be extremely regular, its layout characterized by the intersection of streets at right angles, to form rectangular blocks (*insulae*). Excavation has only unearthed the eastern part of the Decumanus Maximus, the ancient city's main street, which runs east-west. The south side of this street has both shops and patrician homes facing onto it; the most beautiful example is without doubt the House of the Bicentenary, so called because it was

Details of wall decoration: medallion depicting satyr and bacchante

View of Cardo IV with House of the Latticework

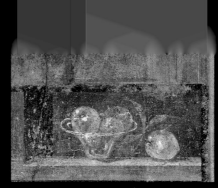

discovered in 1938, two hundred years after the discovery of Herculaneum.

As for the streets running north-south (*cardines*), which all follow the natural slope of the terrain, it is interesting to examine the various types of houses along Cardo IV. Proceeding along the street from the city gate, we first pass a few panoramic houses, i.e. patrician homes of Samnite design, such as the House of the Bronze Herm and the House of the Wooden Partition.

The Forum and the large public buildings next to it represented the heart of the city.

The south sector is dominated by the great panoramic houses, such as the (so-called) House of the Inn, the House of the Mosaic Atrium and the House of the Deer. These dwellings combined the advantage of remaining close to the city center with that of possessing large peristyles and gardens, like the suburban villas, and they exploited the natural lie of the land (which rises here before dropping precipitously down to the sea) in order to create living rooms and panoramic terraces with spectacular views over the sea.

In its final phase, the city developed beyond the walls, as they lost their defensive purpose after the imposition of peace by Augustus (*pax augusta*): suburban villas then sprung up towards the sea and in the surrounding countryside, one example of which is the Villa of the Pisones (or Villa of the Papyri), a sumptuous, patrician dwelling discovered between 1750 and 1765, containing a collection of sculpture and a library of papyri, among other things; in 1986, its

House of the Stags, atrium: head of Hermes
Mosaic panel of Neptune and Amphitrite

exploration was resumed down the shafts sunk in the Bourbon period, with a view to completing the excavation and recovering the
whole library.

HOUSE OF THE MOSAIC ATRIUM

This is a patrician house, typically Italic in design, with rich painted
decoration. It is named after the mosaic paving, in large black and
white squares, which adorns its entrance hall and atrium.

Statue of drunken Hercules, in the garden of the House of the Deer

House of the Mosaic Atrium, reconstruction

Unfortunately, the mosaic was badly corrugated at the time of the disaster, due to the yielding of the substrate to the pressure of the engulfing mud.

The *tablinum* is divided by pilasters into three aisles, of which the central one is the tallest. Next to this complex lies a garden surrounded by a windowed portico, with living quarters opening off it; beyond this is a large, luxurious dining room with adjoining rooms which face out onto a covered loggia and a panoramic terrace overlooking the sea.

Wooden cradle from
House of the Mosaic Atrium

Paestum

Paestum, the ancient city of Poseidonia, was founded by Greeks from Sybaris in around 600 BC. The city boasted a remarkably advantageous geographical position: it lay close to the sea, at the meeting point of the roads to Campania and to Southern Italy. While the settlers of Poseidonia were building their first dwellings and places of worship, such as those of which the foundations are still visible near the Temple of Ceres (towards the southeast), they also dedicated a sanctuary at the mouth of the River Sele to Hera, the most venerated divinity in the colony (and also in the Greek motherland). Near this sanctuary there arose magnificent temples, dec-

(left) Urban sanctuary of Hera: the "Basilica" and the "Temple of Neptune"

(right) Curia, interior

orated with exceptional sculpture (now in the museum) and containing a wealth of votive offerings.

In the 5th century BC, the city underwent a period of extraordinary splendor, judging by the quality and quantity of the monuments. In the second half of the 5th century BC, a new political situation was created by the constant menace of the Italic populations who had been growing in social and military importance. Towards the end of the century, major cities of Campania such as Capua, Cumae and Naples fell to the Samnites. Poseidonia was occupied by groups of the same ethnic background, but who have gone down in history as the Lucanians (the ancient region south of the Sele was to become known as Lucania). Once again, the information is derived from Strabo, but the chronology is obtained from archaeological finds. This event (a full-scale occupation, following a mili-

tary defeat) probably took place towards the end of the 5th century BC, given the sudden change in burial rites which apparently took place during that period. The simple and severe tombs of Greek tradition disappear and are replaced by tombs with decorated coffins and a wealth of vases (in addition to weapons in the tombs of men and jewelry in the tombs of eminent women). All of the 6th century BC is dominated by this new situation, which gives rise to extremely interesting cultur-

Sanctuary of Hera at the mouth of the Sele metope showing (left downwards):

Heracles carrying the Kercopes hanging from a pole

The murder of Aegisthus by Orestes

Metope showing a centaur

Heracles kills the giant Alcyoneus

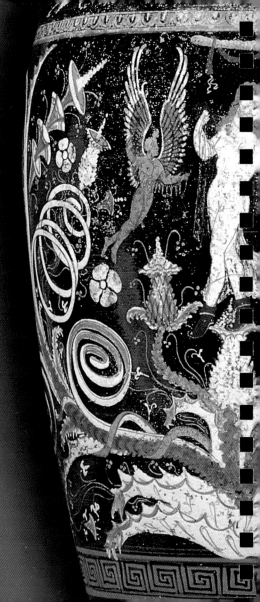

al and social patterns, producing the fusion of Greek and Italic cultures commonly referred to as Italiot.

Between the years 335 and 331 BC Alexander the Molossian, King of Epirus and uncle of Alexander the Great, was invited to Italy by the inhabitants of Taranto to fight the Lucanians and advanced to the foot of the walls of Poseidonia, imposing his authority on the city. But this was only a passing phase, ending in the tragic death of the Epirot monarch. At the same time, the power of Rome began to make itself felt in the south of the Italian peninsula. Unfortunately, we know nothing of the crucial events which marked the final decades of the 4th and early decades of the 3rd centuries BC. We do know that in 273 BC, while Rome was at war with Taranto and Pyrrhus, a Latin colony was founded at Paestum. It is certain that the city had acquired the name Paestum by this time, as it also appears on its coins (and it is possible that the Italic name had also been in use previously).

The inscriptions and monuments depict the profound Latinization of the city. The great temples remained intact, but the city itself underwent radical transformations in plan, with the creation of the forum area and the Latin colony's civil and religious monuments. During the Second Punic War, Paestum was such a steadfast ally of Rome that it received praise in the Senate, along with the 17 other Latin colonies who had refused any aid to the Carthaginians;

Amphora by the "Aphrodite painter": the goddess is depicted between two Cupids, surrounded by a sumptuous decoration of flowers, leaves and scrolls

" Diver's Tomb", detail depicting the group of the so-called "lovers"

and, as if that were not enough, we learn from Livy that the Senate of Paestum had, at the height of the war, voted to send Rome some golden vases (evidently the city treasure and temple artefacts). The Senate thanked Paestum but did not accept them. Nevertheless, Paestum probably felt the effect of the general crisis that struck southern Italy in the following centuries (2nd-1st centuries BC), a social crisis that led to the economic decline of the cities, now reduced to insignificant villages, and also to the neglect of the farmland and the birth of the *latifundia* (large estates).

Some signs of vitality are perceived in the Augustan period, as may be seen from the modest increase in the building sector. During the reign of Vespasian (AD 70) a colony was founded in Paestum under the name of Flavia (the imperial family name), made up of veterans of the Praetorian Fleet formerly based at Cape Misenum.

The city continues to furnish traces of a now fairly stable existence spanning the Imperial Roman era. A steady decline set in, starting from the 5th-6th centuries AD, when the inhabited part of the city shrank to the northern section (as the highest area, it protected its inhabitants from the health hazards emanating from the marshland that was slowly invading the southern area). A small nucleus of inhabitants closed ranks around the Temple of Ceres, the only one of the great temples converted into a Christian church, and buried their dead amongst the ruins of the ancient Greek and Roman city. In the Middle Ages, Paestum was the seat of a Bishopric. It should be mentioned here that there is some question as to the nature of the city's existence in this period, about which so little is known. This is due to the lack of interest shown by specialists, until relatively recently, in the city's medieval artefacts. We therefore expect future research to throw some long-overdue light on this problem. At some uncertain point (8th or 9th century AD) the inhabitants finally abandoned the city, as it had been invaded by marshland. They took refuge in the nearby mountains and founded the town of Capaccio. There they established the Christian cult of Our Lady with the Pomegranate, a cult which retains the iconographic and devotional features of the Greek goddess Hera, who was always depicted with a pomegranate. This is one of the most striking examples of a pagan cult carried over into Christianity. Although the Court of Naples already knew of the site of Paestum in the 16th century, it was only in the 17th century that the cultural establishment "rediscovered" Paestum, ushering in the era of visitors from all over Europe coming to admire the ruins.

"...Paestum is the last and most splendid image which I shall bring north with me, intact" (J.W.V. Goethe, *Journey to Italy*, Naples 17 May 1787)

Poseidonia (known as Paestum from 273 BC onwards) was girded by mighty walls (the fortifications of which are still virtually intact and are one of the best-preserved examples of ancient military architecture) and exhibited a more or less pentagonal city plan, divided into rectangular blocks, with two main streets crossing at right angles.

The heart of the city was dominated by the grandiose Greek temples standing in the sacred precinct, the same area

later occupied by the forum in Roman times. 18th- century scholars mistakenly identified the temples as the Basilica, the Temple of Neptune (both located in the forum) and the Temple of Ceres (in the northern sector). Actually, archaeological investigations have shown that the first two were consecrated to Hera, and the other to Athena. The most ancient temple is the so-called Basilica (mid-6th century BC); unmistakable evidence of its Archaic origin is provided by the odd number of columns across the front (nine, with eighteen down the long sides), their distinct entasis in the center and the marked bulging of their capitals. Between 510 and 500 BC the Temple of Ceres was built, a hexastyle peripteros (six columns across the front) with 13 columns down the long sides. Its highly elegant architectural design featured Doric columns for the *peristasis* (the external colonnade) and Ionic capitals for the *pronaos* (porch in front of the cella).

The so-called Temple of Neptune, the latest of Paestum's great temples, dates back to the mid-5th

Temple of Neptune, view from the north-east; in the background, the Basilica

Temple of Neptune, detail of interior

Temple of Neptune, view from the south-east

South portico of the Forum

Terracotta statue of the goddess Hera with pomegranate (5th century BC)

century BC, and it is one of the most successful executions of Doric architecture in the West. The building is hexastyle, with 14 columns down the long sides, and is Classical in design, as shown by its similarity to the Parthenon. Further evidence of the Greek period is provided by the identification, not far from the Temple of Ceres, of the area of the Agora, the center of political and commercial life in Poseidonia. The underground Sacellum, one of the earliest monuments in the life of the agora, may be identified as a *heroon* (i.e. the mausoleum of someone posthumously celebrated as a hero); in it were found eight bronze vases containing honey, an Attic black-figure vase from the late 6th century BC and five iron spears arrayed on two adjacent blocks to form a table-like structure.

Recent studies have shown that Poseidonia's Greek agora was, during the Roman period, initially a partially abandoned area on the outskirts of the city, where buildings were subsequently constructed (mainly private homes). The new political and administrative center, the Forum, was created further south.

To the east of the former agora is a large circular building dating back to the Classical age: the Ekklesiasterion (the assembly hall of all those adult, male citizens entitled to take part in political life). Further to the south lies the Amphitheater (built in two successive phases, in the 1st centuries BC and AD). To the west is the sacred precinct with the large Piscina (long thought to be a gymnasium, this was in fact an important sanctuary dedicated to the worship of a fertility goddess). Next is the monumental area of the Forum, with those buildings typical of political and economic functions, such as the so-called Curia (this building with three doors and an *exedra* inside, surrounded on three sides by a covered portico, actually responds more to the characteristics of a basilica, the place where justice was administered), the Comitium (this circular building for the election of magistrates was erected by the first generations of Latins to inhabit Paestum, in 273 BC) and the Macellum (the covered market).

The Museum of Paestum is also of great interest: designed principally to house the rich collection of metope sculptures found at the Sanctuary of Hera at the mouth of the Sele, it also contains monuments from the Necropolis, including the remarkable Tomb of the Diver (so-called), a box-like tomb built of four slabs of limestone and a flat lid, decorated with mural paintings on its inside walls. Both the burial treasure and the style of the painting date back to the 5th century BC. There are also a good number of Lucanian tomb paintings dating back to the 4th century BC, so identified by their style of composition, typical of the culture and ritual practices of the Italic world.

HOUSE WITH PISCINA

This is one of the most spacious houses in Roman Paestum, with its pool and large dimensions. The house originally extended to the front of the block. Excavation has shown that, perhaps as the result of an inheritance, the house was divided in two and the pool was filled in and replaced with a peristyle of brick columns faced with stucco, which have now been restored and give a good idea of the portico occupying the space of the former pool.

The House with Piscina, reconstruction

Athenaion ("Temple of Ceres"), detail of east colonnade

Tomb of the Winged Victories, detail of a Victory

Woman's tomb from the Laghetto necropolis:
details of the painted decoration on the south slab,
depicting wounded duellers

THE "TEMPLE OF CERES"

As we enter the archaeological area through the gate opposite the so-called
Temple of Ceres, we see the ruins of a portico, the temple altar and, in the
background, a column set upright again after a modern restoration and
incorrectly called a "votive column". The Temple of Ceres was in fact dedicated to the goddess Athena (the names of the temples, as well as those of
the city gates date from the 18th century, the time of the first travelers, and
are entirely without foundation). Only archaeological studies carried out
since the beginning of the 20th century have thrown any light on this
and other problems concerning the ancient city. Numerous terracotta figurines of Athena with helmet and shield were found
among the temple's votive offerings. We should also take into
account a Latin inscription which proves that the temple
was dedicated to Minerva in Roman times.
The temple, probably erected around the year 500 BC,
has a very refined architectural structure: a Doric peristyle (or external colonnade) with six columns across the
front and rear and thirteen down the sides. The pediment (the triangular part crowning the front) had two
raking cornices but no horizontal cornice, and a coffered
stone roofing that is one of the earliest known examples of
this type. There were also stone lion-headed water-spouts
and a sandstone moulding over the architrave.

The brick restoration of the pediment was done during the last century and is soon to be dismantled. Entering the temple, we find ourselves in the spacious *atrium* of the *pronaos* or antechamber, which had Ionic columns and capitals (the combination of Doric and Ionic elements is an original aspect of this building). Two of the Ionic capitals were found during the 1948 excavations and are now in the museum, along with the water-spouts and other decorative architectural elements of the temple. If we look carefully at the south peripteral colonnade, we notice the remains of tombs which are a sure indication that the temple was transformed into a Christian church. In the Middle Ages, the space between the columns was walled up and the building was adapted to Christian worship by the small group of inhabitants who had taken refuge here, on the highest ground of the city.

We then follow a well-conserved Roman road, paved with basalt stones, which crosses what was a built-up area in Roman times and the city's Agora in the Greek period.

(background) Museum of Paestum:
Tomb 86 of the Andriuolo necropolis, known as
the "Tomb of Winged Victories": scene with
"Return of the Warrior"

Museum of Paestum: Satue of enthroned
male divinity (Zeus?), executed in
polychrome terra-cotta

In its earliest history, Sicily was inhabited by three peoples of different origin: The Elymni (probably local), the Sicani (who may have originated from Iberia) and the Siculi (of Italic origin); the latter had crossed the Straits of Messina from the mainland and pushed the Sicani and

Ancient Sicily

the Elymni into the westernmost part of the island. Archaeological discoveries have confirmed the existence of very ancient trade links between Sicily and the Minoan and Mycenean worlds; these led to the later colonization of the island by the Greeks, who founded several settlements between the 8th and 6th centuries BC.

These new colonies quickly disrupted the Phoenician system of coastal trad-

(left) Selinunte, Temple E

(right) Segesta, Doric Temple, detail of colonnade

ing posts, and so the Phoenicians also started founding settlements of a colonial type, through which they could at least control the western part of the island. So it was that Sicily came to be divided in half, into the Phoenician sphere of influence on the west side (soon to be replaced by Carthage), and the Greek one on the east side. The origin of Sicily's Greek colonies is known to us from writings of the Athenian historian Thucydides: first Naxos was founded by the Chalcidians (734 BC), then Syracuse by the Corinthians (733 BC), Megara Hyblaea by the Megarians (728 BC), Gela by the Rhodians and Cretans (690 BC), Zancle (Messina) by the Cumaeans and the Eubaeans (730 BC) and Himera by the Chalcidians (648 BC).

There were also important secondary colonies, such as Selinunte (founded by Megara Hyblaea in 628 BC) and Agrigento (founded by Gela in 581 BC). Almost all of the Sicilian Greek cities went through a period of government by tyrants: Syracuse, for example, achieved moments of great prosperity and substantial territorial gains, first under Gelon and then under Dionysius I and II, with the creation of various military strongholds and an aggressive policy towards the local populations. There was a greater degree of Hellenization and political unification in Sicily than in the other colonies of Magna Graecia; indeed, it was the Sicilian Greeks who beat the Carthaginians at the Battle of Himera in 480 BC, and the Etruscans at Cumae in 474 BC. The Syracusans also made repeated attempts to unite the Greek element present on the Italic mainland: between the 5th and 4th centuries BC, Dionysius extended the area of Syracusan influence into Magna Graecia; between the 4th and 3rd centuries BC, Agathocles extended his own rule

Segesta, detail of Doric temple

throughout the whole of Sicily, and was the first tyrant to assume the title of king (*basileus*). Under Agathocles, the constant struggle against the Punic people, hitherto directed against their colonies, was finally aimed at Carthage itself; this line of warfare was continued in 278 BC by Agathocles's son in law, Pyrrhus, king of Epirus, who also had to defend himself against the new threat represented by the Mamertines, Campanian mercenaries who, having occupied Messana (as Messina was now named), undertook incursions into the south of the island. But another power was getting ready to replace Syracuse in the countering of Carthage: Rome.

In 263 BC, the new tyrant of Syracuse, Hieron II, in response to the now menacing presence of the Romans off the coasts of Sicily (a presence occasioned by the Mamertines), concluded a treaty of alliance with Rome, to which he remained faithful, and guaranteed the independence of his kingdom (limited to the area under the direct control of Syracuse) after Rome's victory over Carthage at the end of the First Punic War (241 BC).

After Hieron's death, the pro-Carthaginian faction gained the upper hand, which led to the downfall of Sicily's last autonomous Greek state (212 BC), when the Roman general Claudius Marcellus besieged and sacked the city.

After the Roman conquest, Sicily was organized as a province. It suffered further in the events of the third and last Punic war (149 BC), in the slave revolts in 137 and 104-101 BC and in the civil wars which marked the last phase of the Republic, and only acquired its definitive configuration under the emperor Augustus, remaining virtually unaltered until late Imperial times. From the 3rd century AD onwards, property was gradually concentrated into the hands of a few, with the consequent birth of the large estate (*latifundium*), the gradual decline of the urban centers and the creation of luxurious country homes. The conquests of the Vandals and the Goths, and then the Byzantines, with Belisarius's reoccupation in AD 535, perhaps represented Sicily's least prosperous period, which ended with the Arab conquest.

Bouleuterion female divinity, 3rd century BC

FROM THE SPLENDOR OF THE GREEK TEMPLES TO THE MAGNIFICENCE OF THE ROMAN VILLAS

Impressive ruins still bear witness to the presence of the Greeks in Sicily; these ruins are by no means inferior in grandeur and state of conservation to the archaeological sites of Greece itself.

The architecture of the Sicilian Greek temple buildings was essentially of the Doric order, perhaps because most of the founding colonists came from areas of Doric influence. The Greek colonists also remained faithful to the tradition of their

Agrigento, detail of the Temple of Heracles

Selinunte, view of the Acropolis with Temple C in the background

native land in the question of town planning, with orderly and rational street grids; the streets intersected at right angles, creating elongated, rectangular blocks of uniform proportions. The areas of the city were also strictly divided by function (civil, commercial, religious).

The Greek colony of Selinunte (Selinous/Selinus) is a good example of these features. Founded in the mid-7th century BC by the Sicilian Megarians,

Selinunte, Temple E

It attained great prosperity before it was finally destroyed by the Carthaginians in AD 250. Excavations have brought to light a large center standing on a plateau between two rivers, consisting of the hill nearest to the sea, the acropolis, and another to the north, connected to the former by a ridge. The interior part was organized around two main streets running north-south and east-west, which crossed at right angles. On the hill to the east of the city stood three temples of Doric order, now known by the letters E, F and G, as we are not sure to which divinities they were consecrated.

Selinunte's most colossal temple is Temple G, outranked in size only by the great sanctuaries of Ionia and by the

(right) Selinunte, Acropolis: Temple C

Olympieion in Agrigento. It is "pseudo-dipteral" in structure, i.e. it is built as if it had a double external colonnade, whereas in fact it only has one, but at twice the usual distance from the walls of the cella. There are also several monuments dating back to Greek times in Syracuse, the largest Greek colony in Sicily and the West. The best preserved ones are located in the western part of the archae-

Segesta, interior of Doric temple

Agrigento, Vale of Temples,
Temple of Hera Lacinia

ological area (Neapolis). The most celebrated is the theater, the present structure of which dates back to Hieron II (3rd century BC): It was built on top of a 4th century building, itself of great importance in the history of ancient theater. But perhaps the most evocative site of ancient Syracuse is the Latomiae, the large, underground limestone quarries used to house 7,000 Athenian prisoners in 413 BC. Catania, on the other hand, is the only Sicilian Greek city not to have preserved a single trace of the Greek *polis*, totally obliterated by a perpetual succession of war, earthquakes and the eruptions of Mount Etna.

Founded in 729 BC by the Chalcidians, it soon became one of the island's main centers, and also remained so in Roman times, when the city's earlier plan and monuments were assimilated and interpreted to suit the needs of the new conquerors.

A good example of this phase of transition is the replacement of the Agora by the Forum. Catania's largest Roman monument is the Amphitheater. Of considerable size, there are only partial remains of its arched, outer wall and of the *cavea*, but the circular vaulted passageway which ran around the broad arena is preserved almost in its entirety; this was separated from the arena itself by a platform (*podium*), cased in marble, which is still partially preserved. Proceeding along Sicily's north coast, the only big Greek colony is Himera.

Founded around 650 BC by settlers from Zancle together with Syracusan exiles, it was of strategic importance in controlling shipping in the Tyrrhenian and access to it from the interior and south of the island. Excavations have brought to light two successive regular urban plans, organized on perpendicular axes. The oldest, dating back to the Archaic age, corresponds to the orientation of the sacred buildings, while the more recent one is arranged according to the points of the compass, around a big north-south main street opening out to the north into a large, vacant area, perhaps the agora.

The most distinctive temple building is the Temple of Victory (470-460 BC), a peripteral Doric structure with 6 columns across the front and 14 down the sides, built according

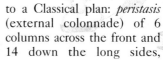

to a classic plan, i.e. with *pronaos* and *opisthodomos* (porches to the front and rear of the cella) which are distyle *in antis*, i.e. with two columns standing between the projecting side-walls. In a context dominated by the Greeks, to the east, and the Carthaginians, to the west, the local populations had no choice but to side with one or the other, in order to survive. This was the case of Segesta, one of the main centers of the Elymni. Long allied to Carthage, it was attacked by Dionysius and Agathocles of Syracuse, but in 260 BC it switched to an alliance with Rome, under whose dominion it regained prosperity.

The most celebrated monument in Segesta is the Doric temple, one of the most famous in Sicily, due mainly to its exceptional state of preservation. It dates back to the second half of the 5th century BC and is built according

Piazza Armerina, Roman Villa: peristyle with fountain

to a Classical plan: *peristasis* (external colonnade) of 6 columns across the front and 14 down the long sides,

Piazza Armerina,
Roman Villa, Mosaic showing:

(left) Great Hunt, detail

Nile scene featuring the capture of a rhinoceros

(right) Figure of Nereid

topped with entablature and two pediments. The theater is also very well preserved, and is important evidence of the phase of transition from the Greek theater to the Roman one, as it was built between the 4th and 3rd centuries BC. While there is therefore ample archaeological evidence of the Greek and Roman periods in Sicily, the period of late antiquity is equally well represented. Indeed, the luxurious Roman villa in Piazza Armerina (Contrada Casale) reflects the decline in urban organization and birth of the *latifundium*, typical of the late Imperial phase. This sumptuous mansion, with its lavish wall decorations and mosaics in the North-African figurative style, was built by a wealthy estate-owner in the first half of the 4th century AD.

The villa was constructed around three main nuclei: the baths (*thermae*), the peristyle courtyard and *ambulacrum* (corridor) and the rooms leading off them, and the *triclinium* with its forecourt, all built on slightly different levels and axes. Piazza Armerina is not an isolated example of private architecture: there is also evidence of similar multi-winged structures in African villas of the same period.

TAORMINA: THE THEATER

The city of Taormina (Tauromenion) was founded in 358 BC by exiles from the destroyed city of Naxos, on the site of a Siculan settlement previously conquered by Dionysius of Syracuse. The city remained part of the Syracusan sphere of influence, and therefore kept out of the events of the First Punic War. During the Second Punic War, as one of the few cities allied to Rome, it was peacefully incorporated into the new order of the Roman province of Sicilia. When Syracuse fell to the Arabs, it remained the principle center of Byzantine Sicily, until it too was conquered in AD 902.

Little is known of the layout of the ancient city. It may have had a double acropolis: one where the Castello stands today and the other at Castel di Mola. The agora (later the forum in Roman times) was probably close to what is now Piazza Vittorio Emanuele. Ancient Taormina's most celebrated and best preserved monument is its theater.

In its current form, it dates back to the Imperial Roman age, but it was certainly first built in an earlier period, perhaps under the rule of Hieron II of Syracuse (mid-3rd century BC), as suggested by an inscription carved on some of the steps, bearing the name of the tyrant's wife (Philistis).

The large *cavea* (109 meters in diameter), reached by a ramp, was partially excavated out of the hillside; around the top, there was a double portico in brickwork, with concentric barrel vaulting and granite columns on the outside. On its inside wall there were 8 openings, corresponding to the 8 stairways dividing the cavea into 9 wedges.

The *orchaestra* (35 meters in diameter) was later converted into an area for gladiatorial contests: pools were built in the middle and there was a high platform (*podium*) all around, behind which ran a semicircular vaulted corridor.

The *scaena* (stage building) had a stage platform (*pulpitum*), later eliminated to enlarge the orchaestra; the *frons scaenae* (stage-building facade) had the usual three gates flanked by niches with columns on either side, and may have been built on two levels (some of its columns were raised in the 19th century); on either side of the scaena were two large rooms, possibly for stage equipment. Behind it are traces of porticoes.

The Theater, reconstruction

AGRIGENTO: TEMPLE OF HERA LACINIA

Agrigento was founded as a colony of Gela in 581 BC. Shortly after its foundation, the city adopted the tyrant system of government. In the 5th century, it adopted a democratic regime and reached its peak of economic prosperity and monumental magnificence, but it was overwhelmed in 406 BC by the advance of the Carthaginians. After various attempts at recovery, Agrigento became the operational base of the Carthaginians in the First Punic War and was sacked by the Romans in 262 BC. It returned to the Carthaginian sphere, but was definitively reoccupied by Rome in the Second Punic War (210 BC).

From then on, it was an integral part of the Roman province of Sicilia and enjoyed a prosperous economic situation. It was taken by the Arabs in AD 829, by which time it had become a small village.

The ancient city was located in a broad, almost rolling valley (known today as the Vale of Temples), sealed off to the

Agrigento, Temple of Concord: seen by night

(opposite page) The Temple of Hera, reconstruction

north by two hills (Girgenti to the west and the Rupe Atenea to the east) and to the south by a continuous rocky ridge, the Hill of the Temples; the valley was also delimited by two rivers, the Akragas (now San Biagio) and the Hypsas (Sant'Anna) which flow into each other and reach the sea at the point of the ancient port (*emporion*).

There aren't many monumental remains on the two northern hills. The famous temples stand out in profile along the crest of the southern ridge. Their names are completely imaginary, apart from that of the Olympieion (the Temple of Olympian Zeus). The easternmost temple is the so-called Temple of Hera Lacinia. This is a Doric building from the mid-5th century BC; it is peripteral (i.e. with an external colonnade), with 6 columns across the front and 13 down the sides. Partially restored, it is Classical in plan, with *pronaos* and *opisthodomos* (porches to the front and rear of the *cella*) which are distyle *in antis*, i.e. with two columns between the projecting side-walls. In the thick wall between the pronaos and the cella are carved two stairways leading up to the roof, a common feature of Sicilian temples, especially those of Agrigento. In Roman times, the marble tiles of the roof were replaced with terracotta, and the ramp leading up to the east front was added. In front of this stands the altar.

Detail of Temple of Vulcan in Agrigento